CAREERS FOR KIDS

When I Grow Up I Want To Be...
Children's Jobs & Careers
Books Edition

**A career is an individual's
journey through learning, work
and other aspects of life.**

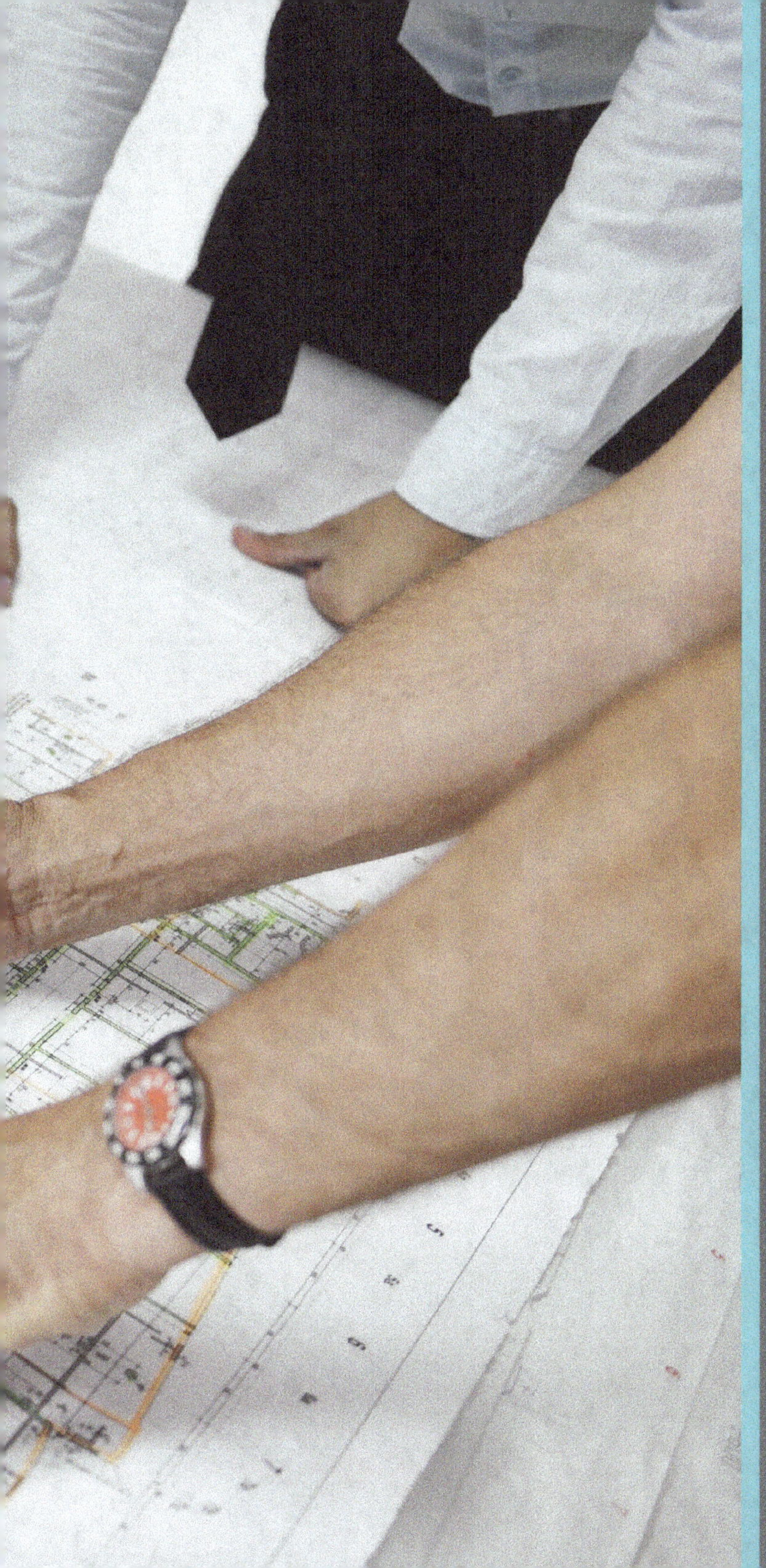

Architects design homes, office buildings, schools, hospitals, sports arenas, shopping malls and so much more.

An architect
must undergo
specialized training
consisting of
advanced education
and a practicum
for practical
experience to earn
a license to practice
architecture.

A computer
programmer
creates the code
for software
applications and
operating systems.

Sometimes programmers use special software which helps them to make programs, such as IDEs, and sometimes they use simpler software, called a text editor, which only gives them a place to type.

cript>
der">
ade </h2>
u pieredze un 30 realizēti projekti</p>

A lawyer is
someone who
practices law.
We need lawyers
because laws are
sometimes so
complicated and
hard to understand
that it takes a lawyer
to figure them out.

Lawyers work in
different settings.
Some work by
themselves,
while some work
in law firms.

Doctors make
people healthier.
Doctors use science
to figure out what is
making people sick.

Becoming a doctor requires more training than most other jobs. They typically hold a college degree in medicine.

英文
English
數學
athematics
常識
ral Studies
其他
Others
交通訊

Teachers teach children to read, write, do math, and much more. Teachers try to make their lessons easy to understand. They teach things in different ways so that different students can learn in the way that is easiest for them.

You must have a college degree to be a teacher. All teachers in public schools must have a teaching certificate, which is a license to teach.

Accountants prepare, analyze, and verify financial records for individuals, businesses, and the government.

People with accounting jobs understand information systems and are skilled at working with computers to gather, report, and interpret information.

Civil Engineer executes the design of the buildings/ structures on site considering the factors of structural stability and other technicalities of the construction process.

Civil Engineering focuses mostly on the physics that enable a building to stand tall for decades and more.

Anyone who picks up a camera can consider themselves a photographer but it takes a lot of practice, creativity, and knowledge about cameras, lighting, scenery, and much more to actually become what most would call a true photographer.

Only the most
skilled and
talented - who have
good business
sense - maintain
long-term careers.

Veterinarians take care of sick and injured animals. They also perform surgery and give medicine.

Vets work in many different places. Most vets who take care of animals work in small clinics and hospitals.